THE CROSSROADS OF ADULTERY

A JOURNEY OF REPENTANCE AND FAITH

KEVIN THUMPSTON

Published by White Blackbird Books, an imprint of Storied Publishing

Permission requests and other questions may be directed to the Contact page at www.storied.pub.

ISBN: 978-1-951991-12-8

Cover design by Sean Benesh

Edited by Doug Serven and Madeleine Dorst

PRAISE FOR THE CROSSROADS OF ADULTERY

With the heart and skill of a seasoned pastor, Kevin applies the healing balm of the gospel to the gaping wounds left by adultery. This book lays out a clear and compelling pathway toward repentance and restoration, every step illuminated by God's redeeming grace. It will be a go-to resource as I counsel couples recovering from adultery.

Brian Walker
Pastor, Lake Morton Community Church
Counselor, Anchored Hope Biblical Counseling

In this wisdom-rich book based on Psalm 51, Kevin Thumpston offers us his heart—the heart of a pastor who cares deeply for men (and their wives and children) who are suffering through the throes of heartbreak, isolation, and suffering that adultery causes in marriage. While confronting adultery head-on, Kevin's book also, with dignity and grace, offers men a hope for the future that is found in Christ alone.

Steven M. Hays
Associate Professor of Business, Columbia International University

In today's society, family values are under attack. There are increasing venues for temptation, busier schedules, and more distractions that can lead to adultery. Adultery is a hard topic to discuss but affecting families at their fundamental roots. Kevin courageously tackles this difficult subject with the application of scriptural wisdom and God's mercy. This book provides biblical based evidence for dealing with and healing from adultery when it occurs. Through Kevin's words, he guides the reader with step-by-step practical strategies for navigating the future after adultery. Kevin refers the reader back to the quintessential guide book for dealing with elements of a broken world, God's Word.

Katie Marie Chambers
Adult/Child & Adolescent/Forensic Psychiatrist

As a pastor and counselor, I'm constantly confronted with the devastation left by affairs on marriages, families, and the larger community of the church. In *The Crossroads of Adultery*, Kevin Thumpston invites men to the road less traveled. One road is marked by selfishness and isolation, the other by repentance and faith. Kevin points all of us to the Gospel of Jesus Christ and the good news that provides real hope for couples as they walk the journey of healing. Through Biblical insight, and pastoral experience Kevin encourages men at the many crossroads after an affair. He reminds us that as we grow in repentance we more clearly see our Heavenly Father's mercy and grace.

Michael Coggin
Director of Care, Redeemer Community Church
Director, Karis Counseling Services

With honesty and transparency, and a willingness to call out the blind spots in our lives and point to the road less traveled of repentance and faith, Kevin connects the Bible's

pastoral integrity regarding sexual sin and the truth of its inevitable fallout, to the hope-filled promise of the gospel to renew and restore even the most broken things in this world through the saving grace of Jesus Christ.
Adam Williams
Pastor, Rivercrest Presbyterian Church

A great resource for counselors and pastors to use when a Christian couple has that panicked moment of an affair revealed. Kevin Thumpston makes sin and forgiveness easy to understand and practical without watering down the fullness of the Gospel or the implications of sin. Regardless if the marriage is repaired or not, the husband will surely be pointed to Christ through this book.
Kayleigh Eswara
National Certified Counselor, Licensed Professional Counselor

Scripture is given to be a light to our path in a world filled with darkness. Thumpston has given us a great gift here—an illuminating walk through one of the most beautiful passages about confession, repentance, and hope, faithfully applying it to the catastrophe of infidelity. Get it and keep it handy. There is a way forward.
Russ Ramsey
Pastor, Christ Presbyterian Church Cool Springs
Author, the *Retelling the Story* Series

If you are "the man" or know "the man" who has absolutely blown it in his marriage, pick up this book and start reading about how serious God's grace is for serious sinners. This book does not promise to fix your broken marriage, and it doesn't guarantee that your wife will forgive you; but it does remind you of the promise of God to "forgive iniquity, transgression and sin" and to "cleanse you from all unrighteousness" if you come to him in honest and full confession. This is a book for the adulterer, the struggler, the wife, the counselor, the pastor and the friend who want to bring sexual sinners back to see *"the Lamb of God who takes away the sin of the world."* If David could find grace in his time of need, so can you when you come in the humble repentance described in these pages and based on David's prayer in Psalm 51. May the Spirit who convinces us of sin give you the strength to see more deeply God's unfathomable and all-sufficient grace; and to know how wide, long, high and deep is the love of Jesus, the Friend of Sinners.

Kent Suits
Pastor, Church Planter, ChristCommunityBL.com

Pastor Kevin Thumpston stands at twelve crossroads of the heart that men who have committed adultery take and wisely and winsomely calls them to the way of Christ: a full confession of their sin and full embrace of the grace of Jesus. This is pastoral care at its best—accessible (it is eminently readable), biblical (it is grounded in Scripture), experiential (it lays bare the twisting and turning of the psyche, the pull of isolating shame, the bent towards defending and pitying self), and Christ-saturated (Jesus is the Defender, Hero and Rescuer in each chapter). Like puritan pastors of old, Kevin is a shepherd of the heart.

Jason Dorsey
Pastor, Redeemer Redmond

The Crossroads of Adultery is a rich and valuable book for any man who believed the lie that a better life could be found in the arms of another woman. Little did he know when he stepped onto that path it would cost him his life. Kevin weaves godly grace into the life-altering destruction of an affair by showing the new road, the road least traveled, of repentance and renewed faith in Christ. It is written by a pastor who has journeyed that road with far too many, so he has the wisdom from God applied to life. If "thou art the man" or a pastor who cares for men who are, read and use this book to disciple men in their journey home.

Tom Wood
Pioneer of Gospel Coaching
Co-author, *Gospel Coach*
President of CMM, Inc.

One day, in the Church Triumphant, adultery will no longer be something the family of God has to endure. Until that day, we will continue to feel the effects of it as it shatters marriages, destroys families, and divides churches. Thankfully, the grace of Jesus Christ is sufficient to overcome adultery's damage! In this book, Kevin Thumpston has done a great benefit to the church by helping men at the crossroads to choose the way of grace and restoration. Full of pastoral insight and godly wisdom, Kevin's winsome gift of discipleship leaps off the pages to meet men where they are as they walk this road. As long as we are in the Church militant, this book will serve the people of God well!

Alex Mark
Pastor, First Scots Presbyterian Church

CONTENTS

ACKNOWLEDGMENTS

First, I want to thank my wife, Andrea, who has been my faithful companion for twenty eight years in marriage, parenting, ministry, friendship, and life. You have been patient, gracious, and forgiving beyond all measure. I love you with an eternal love.

Secondly, I want to thank all the men in my life who have shown me the ropes of being a husband. We have tread many a hill and valley imperfectly together and stayed the course. Thank you for your faithful encouragement and endurance every step of the way.

I also want to thank the many couples that have allowed me to walk with them through the dark night of adultery. I pray you will continue to heal and grow deeper in love with Christ. A special thanks to T & AM for reminding me of God's mercy and steadfast love.

I want to thank all those who previewed the book, especially Dr. Steve Hays. Your tireless editing and keen insight were a true labor of friendship.

Thanks again White Blackbird Books (www.storied.pub)

for giving me another opportunity to minister the Gospel through pen and paper.

Most of all, I want to give praise and honor to the Lord Jesus Christ, who is the faithful Bridegroom and Lover of our souls. All glory be to him forever and ever. Amen

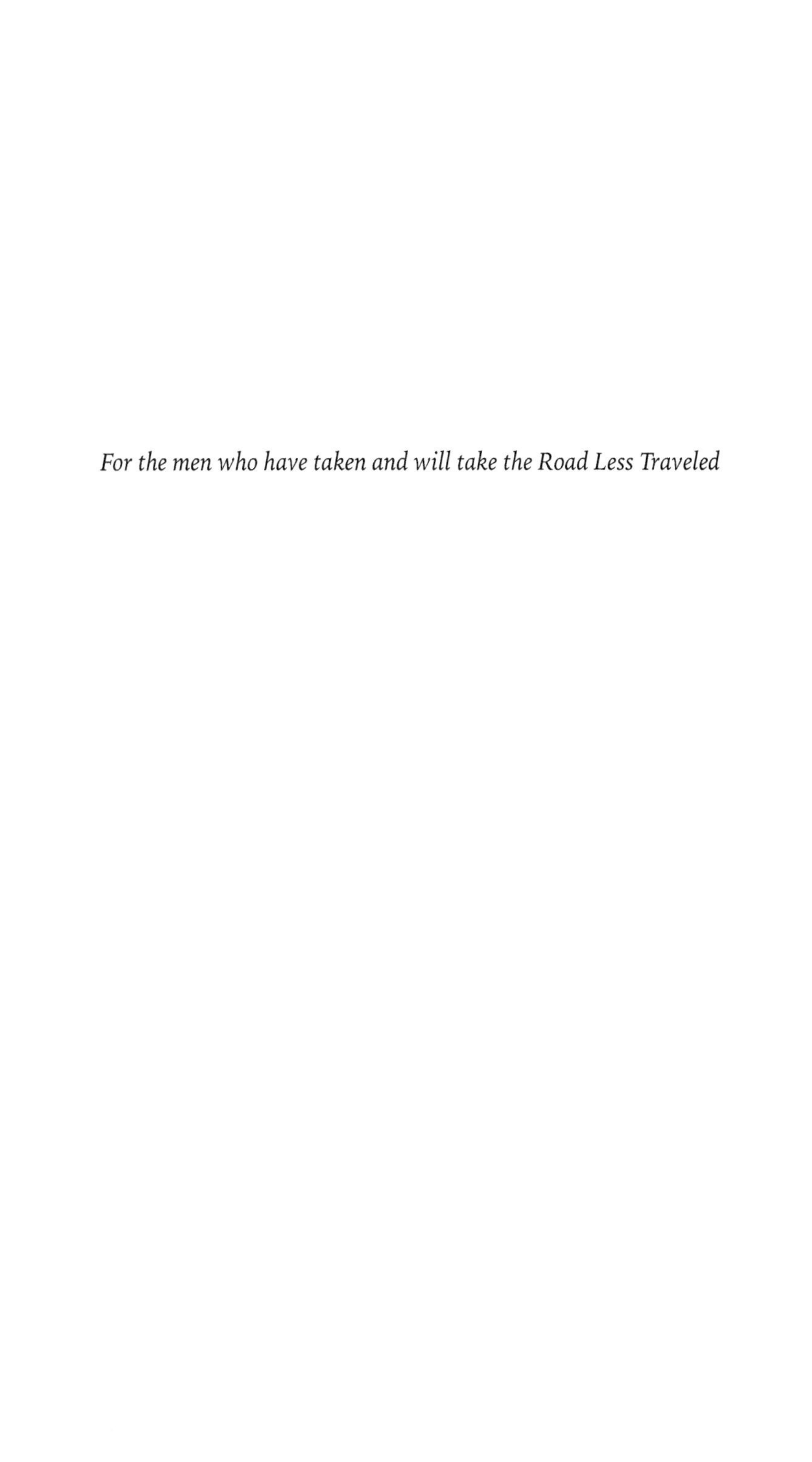

For the men who have taken and will take the Road Less Traveled

AT THE CROSSROADS

Night after night, I kept waking up with Jesus' words ringing in my head: "Leave the ninety-nine to go after the one. Leave the ninety-nine to go after the one." (Matt. 18:12; Luke 15:4)

One of my close friends stopped calling and stopped showing up. He had been isolating himself from church and other relationships for some time. His responses to my texts were brief and distant. It was strange because he and his wife were the life of the party and dearly loved by all. At first, I shrugged it off as social distancing fallout from the pandemic, but to my dismay, I learned he was having an affair. My heart was devastated for him and his wife. He was hiding out in another state, so an elder and I, with our wives, met with his wife to pray diligently for them both. The Lord guided many hard and raw conversations that week, and then I jumped on a plane to go to him.

Leave the ninety-nine to go after the one. In the midst of all our pleading with God in prayer, my friend and his wife experienced a flood of divine kindness and mercy. By God's grace, he chose the road less traveled of repentance and faith.

As a pastor of almost thirty years, I have walked with many friends, family, and church members through very tough situations. Adultery is one of the most difficult to face. The betrayal cuts deep, and the repercussions are pervasive. Most of us don't know what to say or how to help.

With my friend, I was at a loss, but I knew one thing—I needed to go after him.

I wasn't the only one chasing after him. The Hound of Heaven[1] grabbed ahold of my friend and began drawing him back. God took him and his wife by the hand down a road toward each other and reconciliation. Most couples working through an affair quickly realize that it's not a jaunt around the block. It's an arduous journey with many twists, turns, hills, and valleys. It's not a walk back to the way things were, but an expedition forward into uncharted territory. It is one of the hardest treks a couple will ever take, but the view from the heights is glorious and worth every step.

This short book is the result of standing with many friends at the crossroads of adultery. Both men and women come to this spot. This book is written with men in view because I talk to them. There are other books written for women or for both genders, but this isn't one of those.

Some men have chosen to go their own way, but some have taken the road less traveled toward God, wives, and families. Some turned away initially but found their way back on the right path. Others started in the right direction but didn't persevere. Each man must choose the road he will take.

If you are reading this book, it's likely someone who loves you gave it to you. This should encourage you that you are not alone. If you are a husband who has committed adultery, I wrote this book for you. It is also valuable for your wife, even though I didn't write it from her perspective. I designed the book to be a quick read—a starting point in your journey through adultery. It doesn't give you all the answers, and it isn't a substitute for the role of your church, a mentor, and a counselor in your life. It's not a one, two, three-step type of book where if you do these things, then everything will work out just fine. Hopefully, it will be a useful tool to guide your conversations with God and your wife to help prepare your heart to face the many crossroads you will encounter along the way.

Read it. Meditate on it. Pray through it. Invite someone to walk with you through it.

Two roads diverged in a wood, and I—
I took the one less traveled by,
And that has made all the difference.

—Robert Frost, "The Road Not Taken"

OH #$@&%*! WHAT HAVE I DONE?

It's the initial blood-curdling question that pounds in your head on the way home. It's the place of no return. The moment when you realize things will never be the same. You thought you could play with fire, and now your whole world is ablaze. It's the fantasy turned nightmare. And you can't wake up. It's real. You've journeyed down that forbidden path—a flirtatious comment... an emotional connection... an unexpected touch... a secret rendezvous. Now you're *that guy*, branded with the scarlet letter. You are an Adulterer.

Once you crossed the line, something sacred was torn asunder within you, your marriage, and your family. As you look back over the past months, initially you steeled yourself as the victim because something was torn apart long before your infidelity. You told yourself, "She drove me into the arms of another." You tried to justify yourself, convinced that you deserved some happiness.

You retaliated against the voices in your head, saying, "Cut me some slack. I could only take so much." You shut everyone out because no one understood. For months, you craved respect and admiration, but now your corrupted desires have led to sin and whatever you wanted has been tainted. You thought you could hide your sexual misdeeds, plunging yourself further into the darkness.

Lady Folly cast a spell, and you were mesmerized under her seduction. It may have started as a longing for escape through pornography, but you ultimately chose to be all in—mind, heart, and body. You were consumed. Your affair seemed more real than anything else in your life. You toyed with a plan to run away, to forsake your first love and family—all for this other woman.

You settled into living a lie and a double-minded existence. Your efforts to conceal became more demanding, requiring a multiplicity of deception. The web of lies was so extensive you could hardly keep it up. There were days when you wanted to come clean, but shame slammed you back into the corner. Who were you kidding? You didn't want to give up the illicit pleasure. She was your drug, your insanity, your fix to escape monotony. But it was not just the physical; you needed her emotionally. She got you. She listened. You could be yourself without any demands or responsibility. You knew it was wrong, but it felt so right.

Going home became a burden. Tension grew and sincerity waned. Suspicion hung on your spouse's face. Your withdrawal saddened your children, and frustration permeated most of your interactions. But you were numb and needed another fix to feel alive. Your Siren's enchantment beckoned you once again. You pulled out of your driveway in guilt, but your flesh stiff-armed your conscience demanding, "I need this. It's worth it. Just one more time."

Then suspicion grew thick in every conversation. Your story didn't match up. Your lies caught up with you. Instead of confessing though, you deflected and blame-shifted. You did whatever it took to push the inevitable down the road. You knew the truth would come out.

A part of you was okay with that. You began scheming your great escape. You started to convince yourself the grass was greener on the other side. You concluded that so many of your friends were divorced, and they seemed to be just fine.

But something deep within you was disturbed. The warm tender moments of your marriage flashed before you. Your eyes would water as you relived the laughter of your kids as they rushed into your arms, "Daddy's home!" The dreams you made together as a family faded within your heart. You thought about what sort of judgment you'd receive from everyone who knows you. Hearts would be broken, and you were to blame.

You were ashamed, panicked, and disgusted with yourself. It was too late though to turn back, so you thought you might as well enjoy it while it lasted.

Then the day came when the darkness was brought into the light, whether by initiation or confrontation. There was no denying it any longer. Anguish and anger were released with fits of rage and uncontrollable weeping. The bell was rung, and you and your wife came out fists up. The fight over your betrayal was in full fury. It lasted for days, for weeks. The sleepless nights were filled with anxiety, and decision-making was a whirlwind. The tip of the iceberg had hit the ship, but there was so much more hidden in the icy depths of your hearts. Answers were demanded, but diversion prevailed.

You are at a crossroads.

Which road will you take?

Neither road is easy.

One is paved with regret and the other with repentance.

One is hubris and the other humility.

One is coerced by the Father of Lies. The other guided by the Heavenly Father.

One leads to certain severance and the other a hope of reconciliation.

One is fueled by selfishness and the other grace.

Both have a new beginning—one in isolation and the other in community.

My hope for you is you will choose the road less traveled – the road of repentance and faith. I assure you it will make all the difference in your world.

WHAT ARE YOU GOING TO DO NOW?

If you are still reading, you are pondering taking the road less traveled. I commend you for your consideration. I have met many men at this crossroads, both men of faith and men without faith. Some have taken the road less traveled toward God, toward their wife, and toward their family. Others have taken the road away from God, away from their wife, and away from their family.

No matter which path they took, they all had to confront certain decisions of the heart along the way.

Most of these decisions are faced and prayed over in Psalm 51. You may be familiar with this psalm, but if not, it is the prayer of King David after he had abused his power, committed adultery with Bathsheba, and murdered her husband Uriah. The web of lies and deceit had devastating consequences for all involved.

Take a minute and read the backstory of Psalm 51 in 2 Samuel 11:1–12:23, and then read David's prayers in Psalm 51 before we move forward.

During this season of your life, there will be many self-proclaimed counselors offering you advice. Some have good intentions, but the majority will be skewed by their own baggage. Be careful who you allow to speak into your life. God's Word matters far more than anyone else's advice. God said he will send out his Word, and it will not return void but accomplish all he has purposed. Isaiah writes:

> *So shall my word be that goes out from my mouth; it shall not return to me empty, but it shall accomplish that which I purpose, and shall succeed in the thing for which I sent it.* (Isa. 55:11)

Take a few minutes and let God have the loudest voice in your life, if just for this moment.

THE BIBLICAL BACKSTORY & PRAYERS OVER DAVID'S ADULTERY

2 SAMUEL 11-12:23 & PSALM 51

2 Samuel 11

[1] In the spring of the year, the time when kings go out to battle, David sent Joab, and his servants with him, and all Israel. And they ravaged the Ammonites and besieged Rabbah. But David remained at Jerusalem.

[2] It happened, late one afternoon, when David arose from his couch and was walking on the roof of the king's house, that he saw from the roof a woman bathing; and the woman was very beautiful. [3] And David sent and inquired about the woman. And one said, "Is not this Bathsheba, the daughter of Eliam, the wife of Uriah the Hittite?" [4] So David sent messengers and took her, and she came to him, and he lay with her. (Now she had been purifying herself from her uncleanness.) Then she returned to her house. [5] And the woman conceived, and she sent and told David, "I am pregnant."

[6] So David sent word to Joab, "Send me Uriah the Hittite." And Joab sent Uriah to David. [7] When Uriah came to him, David asked how Joab was doing and how the people were doing and how the war

was going. [8] Then David said to Uriah, "Go down to your house and wash your feet." And Uriah went out of the king's house, and there followed him a present from the king. [9] But Uriah slept at the door of the king's house with all the servants of his lord, and did not go down to his house.

[10] When they told David, "Uriah did not go down to his house," David said to Uriah, "Have you not come from a journey? Why did you not go down to your house?" [11] Uriah said to David, "The ark and Israel and Judah dwell in booths, and my lord Joab and the servants of my lord are camping in the open field. Shall I then go to my house, to eat and to drink and to lie with my wife? As you live, and as your soul lives, I will not do this thing." [12] Then David said to Uriah, "Remain here today also, and tomorrow I will send you back." So Uriah remained in Jerusalem that day and the next. [13] And David invited him, and he ate in his presence and drank, so that he made him drunk. And in the evening he went out to lie on his couch with the servants of his lord, but he did not go down to his house.

[14] In the morning David wrote a letter to Joab and sent it by the hand of Uriah.

[15] In the letter he wrote, "Set Uriah in the forefront of the hardest fighting, and then draw back from him, that he may be struck down, and die." [16] And as Joab was besieging the city, he assigned Uriah to the place where he knew there were valiant men. [17] And the men of the city came out and fought with Joab, and some of the servants of David among the people fell. Uriah the Hittite also died. [18] Then Joab sent and told David all the news about the fighting. [19] And he instructed the messenger, "When you have finished telling all the news about the fighting to the king, [20] then, if the king's anger rises, and if he says to you, 'Why did you go so near the city to fight? Did you not know that they would shoot from the wall? [21] Who

killed Abimelech the son of Jerubbesheth? Did not a woman cast an upper millstone on him from the wall, so that he died at Thebez? Why did you go so near the wall?' then you shall say, 'Your servant Uriah the Hittite is dead also.'"
[22] So the messenger went and came and told David all that Joab had sent him to tell. [23] The messenger said to David, "The men gained an advantage over us and came out against us in the field, but we drove them back to the entrance of the gate.
[24] Then the archers shot at your servants from the wall. Some of the king's servants are dead, and your servant Uriah the Hittite is dead also." [25] David said to the messenger, "Thus shall you say to Joab, 'Do not let this matter displease you, for the sword devours now one and now another. Strengthen your attack against the city and overthrow it.' And encourage him."
[26] When the wife of Uriah heard that Uriah her husband was dead, she lamented over her husband. [27] And when the mourning was over, David sent and brought her to his house, and she became his wife and bore him a son. But the thing that David had done displeased the LORD.

2 Samuel 12:1–23

[1] And the LORD sent Nathan to David. He came to him and said to him, "There were two men in a certain city, the one rich and the other poor. [2] The rich man had very many flocks and herds, [3] but the poor man had nothing but one little ewe lamb, which he had bought. And he brought it up, and it grew up with him and with his children. It used to eat of his morsel and drink from his cup and lie in his arms, and it was like a daughter to him. [4] Now there came a traveler to the rich man, and he was unwilling to take one of his own

flock or herd to prepare for the guest who had come to him, but he took the poor man's lamb and prepared it for the man who had come to him." [5] Then David's anger was greatly kindled against the man, and he said to Nathan, "As the LORD lives, the man who has done this deserves to die, and he shall restore the lamb fourfold, because he did this thing, and because he had no pity."

[6] Nathan said to David, "You are the man! Thus says the LORD, the God of Israel, 'I anointed you king over Israel, and I delivered you out of the hand of Saul.

[7] And I gave you your master's house and your master's wives into your arms and gave you the house of Israel and of Judah. And if this were too little, I would add to you as much more. [9] Why have you despised the word of the LORD, to do what is evil in his sight? You have struck down Uriah the Hittite with the sword and have taken his wife to be your wife and have killed him with the sword of the Ammonites.

[10] Now therefore the sword shall never depart from your house, because you have despised me and have taken the wife of Uriah the Hittite to be your wife.' [11] Thus says the LORD, 'Behold, I will raise up evil against you out of your own house. And I will take your wives before your eyes and give them to your neighbor, and he shall lie with your wives in the sight of this sun. [12] For you did it secretly, but I will do this thing before all Israel and before the sun.'" [13] David said to Nathan, "I have sinned against the LORD." And Nathan said to David, "The LORD also has put away your sin; you shall not die. [14] Nevertheless, because by this deed you have utterly scorned the LORD, the child who is born to you shall die." [15] Then Nathan went to his house. And the LORD afflicted the child that Uriah's wife bore to David, and he became sick. [16] David therefore sought God on behalf of the child. And David fasted and went in and lay all night on the ground. [17] And the elders of his house stood

beside him, to raise him from the ground, but he would not, nor did he eat food with them. [18] On the seventh day the child died. And the servants of David were afraid to tell him that the child was dead, for they said, "Behold, while the child was yet alive, we spoke to him, and he did not listen to us. How then can we say to him the child is dead? He may do himself some harm." [19] But when David saw that his servants were whispering together, David understood that the child was dead. And David said to his servants, "Is the child dead?" They said, "He is dead." [20] Then David arose from the earth and washed and anointed himself and changed his clothes. And he went into the house of the LORD and worshiped. He then went to his own house. And when he asked, they set food before him, and he ate. [21] Then his servants said to him, "What is this thing that you have done? You fasted and wept for the child while he was alive; but when the child died, you arose and ate food." [22] He said, "While the child was still alive, I fasted and wept, for I said, 'Who knows whether the LORD will be gracious to me, that the child may live?' [23] But now he is dead. Why should I fast? Can I bring him back again? I shall go to him, but he will not return to me."

Psalm 51

To the choirmaster. A Psalm of David, when Nathan the prophet went to him, after he had gone in to Bathsheba.

[1] Have mercy on me, O God, according to your steadfast love; according to your abundant mercy blot out my transgressions.
[2] Wash me thoroughly from my iniquity, and cleanse me from my sin!
[3] For I know my transgressions, and my sin is ever before me.

[4] Against you, you only, have I sinned and done what is evil in your sight, so that you may be justified in your words and blameless in your judgment.
[5] Behold, I was brought forth in iniquity, and in sin did my mother conceive me.
[6] Behold, you delight in truth in the inward being, and you teach me wisdom in the secret heart.
[7] Purge me with hyssop, and I shall be clean; wash me, and I shall be whiter than snow.
[8] Let me hear joy and gladness; let the bones that you have broken rejoice.
[9] Hide your face from my sins, and blot out all my iniquities.
[10] Create in me a clean heart, O God, and renew a right spirit within me.
[11] Cast me not away from your presence, and take not your Holy Spirit from me.
[12] Restore to me the joy of your salvation, and uphold me with a willing spirit.
[13] Then I will teach transgressors your ways, and sinners will return to you.
[14] Deliver me from bloodguiltiness, O God, O God of my salvation, and my tongue will sing aloud of your righteousness.
[15] O Lord, open my lips, and my mouth will declare your praise.
[16] For you will not delight in sacrifice, or I would give it; you will not be pleased with a burnt offering.
[17] The sacrifices of God are a broken spirit; a broken and contrite heart, O God, you will not despise.
[18] Do good to Zion in your good pleasure; build up the walls of Jerusalem; then will you delight in right sacrifices,
[19] in burnt offerings and whole burnt offerings; then bulls will be offered on your altar.

God included this dark story in his family's history to warn us that no one is above committing adultery and that tempting opportunities will present themselves to all of us. He also included it to reveal the devastating effects of adultery for both the man and woman and to show its ripple effect on others.

God is not afraid to talk about adultery nor to deal with it. We shouldn't be hesitant either. By including David's prayers in Psalm 51, God was and still is encouraging his people to grow in repentance and to understand the power of his grace and mercy toward sinners, even adulterers. The psalms were the hymnal of the church. They were meant to be sung in corporate worship.

Yeah, that's right—the church is supposed to sing about God's mercy and forgiveness toward the adulterer! The sin of adultery is a destructive sin, but it is not an unforgivable one. God's grace is sufficient for you. He will remain faithful even when you are faithless.

The psalms are also meant to be read and meditated on personally in order to deepen your faith, instruct your ways, reveal God's character, and point you to Jesus Christ. Psalm 51 has been treasured by many sinners, including me, because of its humility of confession and its powerful offer of redemption. For adulterers, Psalm 51 should hold a special place in their hearts, because it is a divine companion on the journey down the road less traveled.

As we journey through this psalm, David's prayers will jump out like never before. You will discover twelve crossroads and twelve prayers from the psalm that you must engage along the way. I hope these prayers and words of encouragement will spur you on to follow Jesus into the inmost place of your heart and marriage. Keep reading, and cry out to God through these simple but not easy prayers David prayed himself. You are not alone in this. You can trust the Lord along the road less traveled.

Trust in the LORD with all your heart, and do not lean on your own understanding.
In all your ways acknowledge him, and he will make straight your paths.
Be not wise in your own eyes;
fear the LORD, and turn away from evil.
It will be healing to your flesh and refreshment to your bones.
—Proverbs 3:5–8

Let's look a bit deeper at the twelve crossroads and prayers of David's psalm. I pray you will have the same attitude as Paul did in his pursuit of Christ as you face each of these crossroads. He wrote:

Not that I have already obtained this or am already perfect, but I press on to make it my own, because Christ Jesus has made me his own. Brothers, I do not consider that I have made it my own. But one thing I do: forgetting what lies behind and straining forward to what lies ahead, I press on toward the goal for the prize of the upward call of God in Christ Jesus.
—Philippians 3:12–14

CROSSROAD #1

DISMISSING YOUR SIN OR OWNING THE SEVERITY OF YOUR SIN

Prayer

As the LORD lives, the man who has done this deserves to die…You are the man!… I have sinned against the LORD.
—from 2 Sam. 12:5–13

We are quick to throw the first stone at other sinners. We see the speck in another's eye rather than the plank in our own. You could easily point out your wife's sin, but right now you need to admit and own the severity of your sin.

King David was blind to his guilt in his adultery with Bathsheba until God sent Nathan to confront him. The parable of the rich man and the poor man's little lamb caught David off guard. His response revealed his quick temper to bring swift judgment on another. Compared to the sin of others, we tend to weigh our sin with lighter measures. But once confronted that he was the man, David owned his sin.

Let Nathan confront you today. You are the man!

Unlike society, which has its own hierarchy of acceptability, Scripture declares all sin is deserving of death. We all have sinned and fall short of the glory of God (Rom. 3:23). No one can stand on his own merit before our holy and righteous God.

Sin is when we rebel against God's authority and break his holy law. Adultery in the Old Testament is one of God's commandments that deserves death:

> *You shall not commit adultery.* (Exod. 20:14)

> *If a man commits adultery with the wife of his neighbor, both the adulterer and the adulteress shall surely be put to death.* (Lev. 20:10)

This bad news must shake you to the core before you can embrace the good news of the Gospel. The betrayal of adultery breaks the covenant bond, and it is the sin Jesus says warrants the judicial severance of a marriage. Moses alluded to abuse as another reason for divorce (Exod. 21:10–11, Deut, 21:14), and Paul included the abandonment by an unbelieving spouse (1 Cor. 7:14–15). These are all a breach of the marital covenant, but let's stick to the matter at hand. Adultery cuts a chasm through the vows of trust, purity, and love that unite a husband and wife. It tears at the seams of the heart, mind, body, and soul.

Your adultery culminated with a physical treachery, but it has also tainted your thinking, saturated your emotions, and obscured your faith. Your whole being is stained by the sin of adultery. There is no getting around it—you are the man! Therefore, you must own the severity of your sin before God, within your own heart, and in humility toward your wife. This raw, vulnerable possession of your culpability is the first step on the road less traveled. It's this first step that can silence the storm within you and recalibrate your whole being.

The prophet Isaiah didn't commit adultery, but he had to own his sin—unclean lips. When he stood before our Holy God, he said, "*Woe is me! For I am lost…*"

> *And the foundations of the thresholds shook at the voice of him who called, and the house was filled with smoke. And I said: "Woe is me! For I am lost; for I am a man of unclean lips, and I dwell in the midst of a people of unclean lips; for my eyes have seen the King, the LORD of hosts!"* (Isa. 6:4–5)

Isaiah felt like he was coming apart at the seams, like his whole being was disintegrating. If unclean lips has this kind of effect, how much more so for the sexually unclean man.

In the midst of his affair, one of my friends could not even describe the chaos swirling around in his head—a mental breakdown, an extreme identity crisis due to his sin. Another friend in adultery had such erratic behavior it could only be described as insanity.

The deadly effects of adultery are working within you mentally, emotionally, physically, and spiritually.

The first crossroad is to admit the severity of your sin. It is the only way to calm the storm, the disintegration within you. You will never be able to understand the depth of

Christ's mercy until you see the despicable, destructive nature of your sin.

One wife described the destructive nature of her husband's betrayal as an emotional, spiritual, and physical hurricane of epic proportions. She would catch herself touching physical objects in a room just to make sure she wasn't in a horrific nightmare.

To own your sin is part of what the Bible calls repentance. It is God's kindness that will lead you toward repentance; therefore, you must ask him for it.

So what should you ask for?

First, you must ask God for the strength to turn away from your ongoing sin, to put it to death, and to cut off every tie with this other woman.

Second, you must ask God to reveal the depth of your sin, so you can go deep in your remorse over it.

Third, you have to ask God to turn you around so you can run into the arms of Christ for forgiveness.

Last, you must decide to take the road that leads to life rather than the one that leads to death.

Jesus is the way, the truth, and the life! Ask God to enable you to follow him by taking the initial step of repentance. You can trust the Lord's kindness to deal mercifully with the severity of your sin.

Nathan told David:

> *The LORD also has put away your sin; you shall not die. Nevertheless, because by this deed you have utterly scorned the LORD, the child who is born to you shall die.* (2 Sam. 12:14)

David escaped death, but another had to die. In Christ,

God declares that, despite utterly scorning the LORD and your wife, you don't have to die, but another son had to in your place. God's son, Jesus Christ, died because of your sin. He had to die so you might live. I pray you do not scorn his death by taking the path most traveled—the road of pride. God went to great extremes so you could take the road less traveled of repentance and faith. I urge you to take it.

As you work through each crossroad and prayer from Psalm 51, I have included a personal prayer as an example to help you formulate your own prayer to God. This may require being still before God as he speaks these truths into your heart before you utter a single word.

Don't hold back. Go to God wholeheartedly in prayer.

O holy and righteous Lord,
I bow the knee before you as a man guilty of adultery. I have sold myself into the slavery of infidelity. I gave in–no–I *willingly* betrayed my wife, my family, and you. I chose to break my marriage covenant rather than faithfully uphold my vows. I have lived a lie for so long. I confess that I don't know the way out. I don't have the strength or the endurance to make things right. I need you to take hold of me, my heart, mind, body, and soul. I need your kindness to lead me to repentance. Sever my adulterous relationship. I confess it is wrong. It is sin. I have broken your holy commandments. I have forfeited my marriage rights. I am undone and twisted up in the core of my being.

Turn my heart to you. Turn my heart back to my wife and to my family. I choose to take the road less traveled. I will lean on you and not my own understanding. I will trust you to make my paths straight. Into your hands I commit myself, my wife, and my family. Have your way with me.

In the name of Jesus Christ, the way, the truth and the life,

Amen.

Personal Thoughts, Questions, and Prayers:

CROSSROAD #2

MUSTERING UP YOUR OWN STRENGTH OR CLINGING TO GOD'S MERCY AND STEADFAST LOVE

Prayer

Have Mercy on Me, O God, according to your steadfast love, according to your abundant mercy.
—Ps. 51:1a

The Evil One is the Accuser of the Brethren and the Father of Lies. The first thing he will attempt to do is to distort your thinking about the character of God. He will spew out lies like, "God will never love you as an adulterer. God won't listen to you. His mercy can't cover such heinous sin."

Or the devil will try and convince you: "It's not that big a deal. Everybody is doing it. You can work this out without going to God."

Your own heart will also try to condemn you with whispers of shame and guilt, claiming, "Your wife could never forgive you. How can you even show your face to your family again? You just need to run away."

As you try and go about your daily routine, it will seem that everyone's glances are hot lasers burning right through you. Everything in you will be telling you to turn back to your mistress and away from God and your wife. You must trust God's Word over the accusations. The first days after your initial decision to take the road less traveled are some of the hardest. You cannot do this on your own. You can't muster up the strength needed within yourself. You need the power of God's mercy and love to hold you fast. After Jesus was baptized into his ministry, he was led into the desert and tempted by the devil. His sonship, understanding of truth, and allegiance to the Father were all challenged, but he clung to the Word of God in every attack.

You must do the same. Since Psalm 51 is Scripture, you can use the prayers within it as trustworthy weapons in your fight for faith and your marriage.

This initial prayer from Psalm 51 is the anchor for all the others. It's like repelling into the deepest, darkest cavern you have ever leaned over. You must tether yourself to the abundant mercy and steadfast love of God before the descent.

David armed himself and secured his very being in the character of God. He cried out for God to have mercy on him. Mercy and grace are the loving arms of God held out to sinners. Mercy is God not giving us what we deserve or fearfully expect.

We all deserve his judgment, but out of mercy he offers forgiveness. With the other arm, God offers grace for sinners by giving us what we have not earned. He lifts his heavy hand of wrath from us and extends his hand of favor. He bestows upon us salvation, righteousness, an inheritance, a hope, and his very Spirit. Once he wraps his arms around us, he will never let us go. This is his steadfast love —his covenantal love.

Nothing else can hold you when dealing with sin. In Hebrews, we see there is only one who can be the anchor of your soul:

> *We have this as a sure and steadfast anchor of the soul, a hope that enters into the inner place behind the curtain, where Jesus has gone as a forerunner on our behalf.* (Heb. 6:19–20a)

Jesus has faced sin and death, and he has conquered them on behalf of those who put their trust in him. He has gone before us as a forerunner. In the midst of a storm, a forerunner, a stealthy small boat, was sent into the harbor avoiding the reef and rocks. It was tethered to the ship, and it acted as an anchor until the storm had passed so the ship could safely pull into the harbor. God offers his mercy and steadfast love in Christ to anchor you as you weather the storm of adultery.

This is why he sent his Son Jesus Christ to go before us, to do what we couldn't do for ourselves. God took on flesh and dwelt among us. He was born in weakness, in a shameful town, and in poverty to identify with us in our weakness. He was tempted in every way but was without sin, so he could sympathize with us in our struggle. He was rejected, mocked, cursed on the cross, and shamed by his own people.

And get this! In Hebrews, it is also written he did it all

for the joy set before him. Jesus chose to forego his own temporal pleasure to joyfully give his life for his bride. We read:

> *Therefore, since we are surrounded by so great a cloud of witnesses, let us also lay aside every weight, and sin which clings so closely, and let us run with endurance the race that is set before us, looking to Jesus, the founder and perfecter of our faith, who for the joy that was set before him endured the cross, despising the shame, and is seated at the right hand of the throne of God.* (Heb. 12:1–2)

As we weather the storm and run the race, we are to fix our eyes on Jesus, the founder and perfecter of our faith. He hung on the cross and took our shame for us! He showed us mercy by taking the judgment we deserved. He conquered our sin and the judgment of death and now sits as the victor at the right hand of the throne of God.

Cling to his Mercy! Your victory is in him! His everlasting love will hold you fast! Lean into his mercy and steadfast love by tethering yourself in prayer to Jesus.

O Merciful One and gracious God,
Hold me in your steadfast love. I am weak and fainthearted. I am prone to wander, so tether me to Jesus, the founder and perfecter of my faith. Lord, my heart condemns me, and the evil one is relentless in persuading me to take my eyes off of you. I don't want to believe the lies, but Lord, it is hard to believe you can love me after what I have done, and I confess

I still struggle to turn away from my fleshly desires. I know this struggle will not just disappear, so I need you to give me the diligence to remain dependent on you. At times, I think I can do this myself. Forgive me. As I face the condemning glances, may I remember your merciful gaze from the throne room of grace. God, I know I have a tough race to run. Enable me to throw off every sin that will hinder me so I can endure. I praise you for your steadfast love, for I know I will stumble and fall. Pick me up each time and give me the joy that is set before me and the victory you have secured.

In the name of Jesus Christ, the anchor of my soul, Amen.

Personal Thoughts, Questions, and Prayers:

CROSSROAD #3

CONFESSING JUST ENOUGH OR MAKING A FULL CONFESSION

Prayer

Blot out my transgressions. Wash me thoroughly from my iniquity, and cleanse me from my sin!
—Ps. 51:1b–2

There is a huge difference between worldly and godly grief. Paul helps us see the difference in 2 Corinthians. He writes, *"For godly grief produces a repentance that leads to salvation without regret, whereas worldly grief produces death."* (2 Cor. 7:10)

Worldly grief is the fruit of shallow repentance, and it produces death. When your adultery was revealed, your repentance may have been a true confession of sin, but was it a full confession? Our flesh is only willing to reveal enough of our sin to quiet our nagging, worldly grief and just enough to appease our spouse for the moment. Worldly grief is only a partial confession and not the full confession of true repentance. True repentance confesses all of it without regret.

Even though it is agonizing, your wife wants–and needs–to know the full story of your betrayal. She will also have many, many questions.

I recommend doing this full accounting with a trained third party like a trusted pastor or counselor. This will show her you want her to feel safe and that you welcome accountability. Your heart will convince you the whole story will be too devastating, too shameful, and it will hurt her too much. You will be tempted to only share some of the details of your affair under the false pretense that this is best.

Your confession is going to wound your wife like a firing squad, and you are the one wielding an automatic assault rifle. It is more loving to wound her deeply once than to march her in front of the firing squad month after month as more of your sin is revealed.

Your unconfessed sin is like an assassin sniper waiting to take her out at just the right moment. Each time she finds out you have held back something or lied again, she will feel the excruciating pain of betrayal all over again. If she does proceed, she will do so in mistrust and tremendous fear of what lurks around the next corner. Lasting trust will rarely be regained.

In the psalm, David makes a three-fold full confession.

He begins with his transgressions, the very specifics of his sin of adultery. He asks God to blot out each of them by his mercy. He doesn't hold back and lays it all out before the Lord.

Second, he confesses his iniquity, where he acknowledges his sin wasn't only his outward actions but part of the texture of who he has become. His sin has shaped his character. He doesn't try to fool God or anyone else that he is a good guy, just slipping up this one time.

No, he confesses that he has been an evil and sinful man. His behavior is the outflow of his wicked heart. David doesn't hide under a cloak of self-preservation but admits "I am the Man." He says "I am an adulterer, a betrayer, and a liar!"

Lastly, he confesses that he has totally abandoned his calling as a man, a husband, and a king. He asks God to cleanse him from his sin, which is an archery term. David conveys that he has missed the mark for his life that God intended for him. David chose his own bullseye, to indulge his selfish desires of fleshly pleasure. David has made a full confession of his specific sins, his sinful nature, and his choice to alter the purposes for his life, marriage, and family.

David uses an interesting word when he asks God to wash him thoroughly. This washing is not a rinse in the sink. Its the kneading and beating of clothes on a rock down by the river. Alexander Maclaren described David's request this way: "Wash me, beat me, tread me down, hammer me with mallets, dash me against stones, do anything with me, only be sure these foul stains are melted from the texture of my soul."[1]

You must come clean with everything if you want to have any chance of reconciliation with your wife. You need to confess the specifics of your adultery, any previous infidelity, the texting, emails, calls, visits, and anything that accompanied your betrayal—whatever your wife wants you to tell her.

You also need to confess a godly grief over the man you have become. And your abandonment of God's calling on your life as a man, husband, and father. As you prepare your heart to make a full confession to your wife and family, go to the Lord first. Remember—you are tethered to the mercy and steadfast love of God. Pray for her to be bound to Jesus also. This will be the hardest thing you will ever share and the hardest thing she has ever heard. Go to the Lord in prayer with confidence that he will hear you and blot out your sin, wash the texture of your character, and cleanse you of your sin.

O Heavenly Father, my judge and redeemer,
I am filthy through and through. There is nothing good in me. I have sinned in so many ways with so many selfish intentions. I fear my full confession will be the death of a thousand cuts for my wife. Lord be gracious to her as I wound her deeper than she has ever been before.
Tend to her heart as I pour out the specifics of my transgressions to her. Lord, you know that even my prayer for her flows out of a desire for my own selfish gain. Father, I have chosen to be a man of darkness, a prodigal rather than a man of light, rather than your son. I have made my bed in the graveyard of death and destruction. My identity is so misshapen that I don't even know the extent my wickedness inter-

twines the fabric of my being. I have put myself first before my wife and before my family over and over again. I have forfeited the right of their honor and respect. Lord, I need you to wash me through and through. Leave nothing un-scoured. I beg of you, cleanse me and bend me back in accord with your will and good pleasure.
Through the name and blood of Jesus Christ,
Amen.

Personal Thoughts, Questions, and Prayers:

CROSSROAD #4

SELF-JUSTIFICATION OR ACKNOWLEDGING GOD'S RIGHTEOUS JUDGMENT

Prayer

For I know my transgressions, and my sin is ever before me.
Against you, you only, have I sinned and done what is evil in
your sight, so that you may be justified in your words and
blameless in your judgment.
—Ps. 51:3–4

Along the road less traveled, you will at some point want to divert from the journey of reconciliation with the desire to justify yourself and your actions. As your wife revisits your infidelity over and over, anger and frustration will well up in you.

You'll want to shift the blame. Instead of the issue at hand, you will want her faults to take center stage. You will be tempted to argue that her sin was the cause of your infidelity. Sure, you're not the only cause of your marital struggles, but you are the only one to blame for your adultery.

Your spouse was not the cause—you were lured and enticed by your own desire—"Then desire when it was conceived gave birth to sin, and sin when it was fully grown brought forth death" (modified from James 1:14b–15).

Look at how David continues to pray. He says, "I know *my* transgressions and *my* sin is ever before *me*." He continues to focus on his own sin. He wants to deal with himself first because his sin is ever before him. His agenda is to first get right with God before pointing the finger at someone else. He could have derailed his repentance by focusing on how his wife Michal despised him, or all the stress that his father-in-law Saul caused him, or the weight of responsibility as a king. Instead, he deals with his own heart first and foremost.

He knows he has sinned against God. God alone is his judge.

This doesn't minimize his sin against Bathsheba, Uriah, and Israel. He knows the buck stops with God; therefore, David has no defense to justify himself. You can trust God knows it all, and he will deal with each person accordingly. David doesn't shake his fist at God, as if God is treating him unjustly. He declares that God is justified and blameless in his judgment.

Along the road of reconciliation, God will work in the heart of your wife and reveal to her what she must own for herself. A good biblical counselor will be a helpful guide in this process. Your humility before God and your earnest pursuit of your wife will be two of the means God uses to open the eyes of her heart.

Fight against your desire to sideline your adultery or to make her sin the main issue. There will be time to put all the pieces on the table, but initially, you need to give your wife the necessary time to process your infidelity. If she is a Christian, the Holy Spirit will be working in her heart pointing out areas that she needs to repent of as well. Reconciliation is a supernatural work that God does in both the husband and the wife. It is not a one-way street. Fight against the need to justify yourself by blaming your spouse. Trust and wait on the Lord to do immeasurably more than you can ask or think in both of your lives. We read:

> *I wait for the LORD, my soul waits, and in his word I hope; my soul waits for the Lord more than watchmen for the morning, more than watchmen for the morning.* (Ps. 130:5–6)

Stand before God in prayer as a man who doesn't try to defend himself, but one who accepts that God knows all the angles. He is justified in his words and blameless in his judgments toward you.

O Lord, my judge and my redeemer,
I come to confess that it is hard not to try and justify myself. I am not the only culprit in this fiasco, but please remind me that I am the chief sinner right now. I have a list of accusations compiled in my head against my wife. I have had them stored up for some time now, and at times, I even believe she is the reason I ran into the arms of another. But instead, I

lay my judgments at your feet. I am not her judge, nor am I right to want to administer judgment upon her. You already know this bitterness that still lingers, but I confess it to you now so you can forgive me once again. Lord, the evil I have committed against you is always with me. The tentacles of my adultery seem to be wrapped around every aspect of my life. I can't escape it. Lord, you are the only one who can remove its hold on me because you are the one I have sinned against. Therefore, I wait under your judgment, but I also wait in your Word. Your Word of hope. Your Word promises redemption. I will wait in my Redeemer, the very Word of God who took on flesh. I will wait in the Lord Jesus Christ. I will hide myself in him for you have poured out your judgment upon him in my place, for your Word says you judge the secrets of men by Christ Jesus. May the presence of Jesus cover over my ever-present multitude of sins.

In the name of Jesus Christ, my righteousness and redemption,

Amen.

Personal Thoughts, Questions, and Prayers:

CROSSROAD #5

RELIVING YOUR GUILT OVER AND OVER OR BEING CLEANSED FROM YOUR GUILT ONCE AND FOR ALL

Prayer

Purge me with hyssop, and I shall be clean; wash me, and I shall be whiter than snow.
—Ps. 51:7

There will be days when you feel like a dead man walking. You will feel as if you can never be cleansed from this sin. Your scarlet letter is impaled on your chest. The guilt is like shackles that burden your every step. You have taken up residence on death row, waiting until the imminent day of judgment.

Some nights you can't sleep as you mull over and over how stupid you were to plunge yourself into adultery. You wish you could rewind your life and choose differently, but you can't. You need not stand alone in your struggle with guilt. Communicating this battle to the Lord is essential.

Talking to your wife about this struggle may be useful in her healing.

Take heart as you work through your guilt! God bids the guilty to come with Jesus into his throne room not to be judged but to receive grace and to be cleansed of guilt. Through Christ, he declares that, even though your sins are like scarlet, they shall be as white as snow. Isaiah declares:

> *Come now, let us reason together, says the LORD: though your sins are like scarlet, they shall be as white as snow; though they are red like crimson, they shall become like wool.* (Isa. 1:18)

David went to God in prayer and asked to be purged with hyssop. David felt like a self-inflicted leper that had been declared unclean. He wanted to be washed and cleansed once and for all. He wanted to be brought back into fellowship with God. In the Old Testament ritual, the priest was called to judge between who was clean and who was unclean. Once the priest evaluated the person clean, he would take a hyssop branch dipped in the blood of a sacrifice and sprinkle the person seven times with the sacrificial blood to declare them cleansed. This ritual removed their judgment and gave them a right standing before God (Lev. 13–14). The hyssop branch and the blood from the sacrificial animals were effective during that season of God's redemptive history, but they ultimately pointed to our need for the all-sufficient sacrifice of Jesus Christ.

Christ was fully God and fully man. He was crucified on a cursed tree with outstretched arms to cleanse sinners from their guilt. The blood that poured from his wounds would be God's perfect sacrifice to—once and for all—wash away sin and to declare those who put their faith in him, "Cleansed!"

> *But when Christ had offered for all time a single sacrifice for sins, he sat down at the right hand of God,...And by that will we have been sanctified through the offering of the body of Jesus Christ once for all.* (Heb. 10:10, 12)

As I mentioned previously, adultery is not an unforgivable sin. It can be forgiven by Jesus. How you handle adultery will reveal if you are a believer and follower of Christ. Adultery is one of the reasons Christ took on flesh to die for sinners. If you choose to not follow him in repentance and faith, it reveals much about your heart.

I don't say that to bring condemnation down upon you but to warn you and point you to Christ. You probably know the familiar verse John 3:16, but I want to draw your attention to the verse that comes after it. Jesus didn't come into the world to condemn us but to offer salvation:

> *For God so loved the world, that he gave his only Son, that whoever believes in him should not perish but have eternal life. For God did not send his Son into the world to condemn the world, but in order that the world might be saved through him.* (John 3:16–17)

You need to take the guilt of your adultery to the Lord and be cleansed once and for all. He is the only one who can cleanse your soul and remove your guilt. This is what true love looks like. Jesus took your penalty for sin through his death on the cross. At the same time, he transferred his righteousness to your account. Jesus appeased the wrath of

God by being your sacrifice and substitute. Your guilt has been dealt with in Christ. By faith, you stand righteous in Christ. He is your double cure. As Augustus Toplady's hymn, "Rock of Ages," resounds:

From Thy riven side which flowed,
Be of sin the double cure,
Cleanse me from its guilt and power

When your heart condemns you or anyone else wants to dig up your guilt, let another great hymn pour forth from your soul. Robert Lowry wrote:

What can wash away my sin?
Nothing but the blood of Jesus.
What can make me whole again?
Nothing but the blood of Jesus.

O precious is the flow
that makes me white as snow;
no other fount I know;
nothing but the blood of Jesus.

For my pardon this I see:
nothing but the blood of Jesus.
For my cleansing this my plea:
nothing but the blood of Jesus.

O precious is the flow
that makes me white as snow;
no other fount I know;

nothing but the blood of Jesus.

Nothing can for sin atone:
nothing but the blood of Jesus.
Naught of good that I have done:
nothing but the blood of Jesus.

O precious is the flow
that makes me white as snow;
no other fount I know;
nothing but the blood of Jesus.

This is all my hope and peace:
nothing but the blood of Jesus.
This is all my righteousness:
nothing but the blood of Jesus.

Stand under the cleansing flow of Jesus' blood and be declared, "Cleansed, Not Guilty!"

O my crucified Lord, my perfect sacrifice, I come under the cleansing flow of your precious blood that was shed for me on the cross. Wash me and cleanse me and make me whiter than snow. I put my trust in you as my substitute. I praise you and thank you for dying in my stead, so I might live. I ask you to wash my sin with your indelible grace. Remind

me of your once-and-for-all sacrifice every time guilt creeps back up to condemn me. I know it is only because of you that I can be declared righteous and clean, so give me the strength to stand not on my own but in you. I am washed in your blood.
Nothing can for sin atone: nothing but the blood of Jesus. Naught of good that I have done: nothing but the blood of Jesus.
Amen.

Personal Thoughts, Questions, and Prayers:

CROSSROAD #6

HIDING IN SHAME OR BEING JOYFULLY RESTORED FROM YOUR SHAME

Prayer

Let me hear joy and gladness; let the bones that you have broken rejoice. Hide your face from my sins, and blot out all my iniquities.... Restore to me the joy of your salvation
—Ps. 51:8–9, 12a

If guilt is the relentless right-handed jab to your face, then shame is an uppercut that knocks you off your feet. Together they are the one-two knockout punch. Guilt is the condemnation of what you have done. Shame, on the other hand, is your diminished estimation of who you are.

There will be days you tell yourself, "You are a rotten, good for nothing, cheating scumbag. How in the world can you even get up in the morning?"

Now don't get me wrong; there is a healthy Spirit-filled aspect of guilt and shame that drives us to Christ and knocks us out, so we can awaken with new eyes to see ourselves rightly before our holy and righteous God. But once we have died to it in Christ, we shouldn't come back under its slavery or let anyone shackle us to it again.

Shame causes you to retract from everyone. It locks you up in a prison of isolation and then swallows the key. Shame robs you of any morsel of joy. It leaves you exhausted and numb. Life seems tasteless. You feel like an outcast. You feel like you don't deserve happiness again, nor friendships for that matter. You don't let anyone see, but you find yourself crying more than you ever have before. Your shame takes your breath away and sends you into panic attacks.

When you committed adultery against your wife, you sinned against all the relationships that were intertwined with your marriage, extended family, and friendships. Instead of facing them, you will be tempted to avoid them as much as possible.

You will conclude, "I'm not going to put myself through any more humiliation. It's none of their business anyway." You will even travel outside of your town to shop so you won't bump into anyone.

This is a sign that something deep within you is broken. It's not good for man to be alone. You are created for community—to love others and be loved by them.

The psalmist feels the weight of this brokenness and the ache of shame in his bones. Instead of wallowing in the shame, he cries out to God, "Let me hear joy and gladness; let the bones that you have broken rejoice."

Shame is part of the trauma of adultery for the husband, the wife, and the kids. David realized only God could deal with his shame and give him joy and gladness again. He asks God to restore unto him the joy of *your* salvation. It is God who has saved him, and it is to God whom he must turn to be rescued from his shame. Part of God's salvation is the healing from shame. Your wife and children are heavy laden with shame as well. Pray that God would set them free.

Remember, Jesus endured the shame of the cross for you. He hung naked and exposed for all to see and mock. He endured it for you; therefore, you must hide yourself in Christ. He understands your shame and will walk with you in it. He will never leave nor forsake you.

You will say, "I get that, but isn't the shame Jesus took the shame that believers endure in following him? I deserve my shame for what I have done to my wife and kids. I wasn't following Christ but running away from him. My actions deserve shame. No way Jesus can take joy in mine."

You are right that Jesus doesn't delight in your previous rebellion, but he does take joy in restoring a sinner who turns away from sin and follows him in the present. Jesus will move toward a repentant sinner every time. He will not turn us away. Here's your opportunity!

Follow Jesus on the road less traveled with repentance and faith. He will take joy in walking with you through your shame as you trust him. He will quicken your step and give you a cadence of joy. As Jack Miller used to say, "Cheer up! You're a worse sinner than you ever dared imagine, and you're more loved than you ever dared hope."

Your humility and obedience pave the way for healing in your wife and kids' hearts. Finding joy again requires faith to press into community and to remain honest and vulnerable with others. The psalmist doesn't ask to hide from God but for God to hide his face from his sins and blot out his iniquities. In doing so, he is asking God to draw him into fellowship with the Lord and others.

Shame draws its power in isolation. The secret to conquering shame is humble, honest transparency within community. Hebrews speaks of Jesus not being ashamed to be associated with sinners:

> *For he who sanctifies and those who are sanctified all have one source. That is why he is not ashamed to call them brothers, saying, "I will tell of your name to my brothers; in the midst of the congregation I will sing your praise." And again, "I will put my trust in him."* (Heb. 2:11–13a)

Praying over your shame will probably be a recurring prayer throughout your journey, but I encourage you to put your trust in the Lord again and again and again. Jesus is not ashamed to call you his brother. This should bring a smile to your face, and put joy in your heart.

Bring your shame to Christ. Do not allow it to hold you under its power any longer.

O Lord, my unashamed brother,
I am cut to the core that you are not ashamed of me
and call me brother. May your steadfast love follow
me all the days of my life. Thank you for never
leaving me nor forsaking me even when I want to run
and hide. I confess that I would have hurled shame
upon you at the cross along with everyone else. Oh

Lord, do not treat me as I would you. I beg of you, uphold me in my shame. God, you know the ache in my bones and the deafening silence of my isolation. It's not just my sin that is ever before me, but my shame is like the air I breathe. I can't even look people in the eye. Lift me up and lead me where you would have me go. Guide me toward the people you would have to help me find respite. God, give my wife the joy of your salvation. Heal up the brokenness I have caused. Give her gladness once again. Rescue her from the shame she undeservedly carries. And if it is your will, give us joy and gladness together. May our family be mended through the power of your salvation.

In the name of Jesus, the one who bore my shame, Amen.

Personal Thoughts, Questions, and Prayers:

CROSSROAD #7

SETTLING FOR SHALLOW MODIFICATION OR DELIGHTING IN DEEP TEACHABILITY

Prayer

Behold, I was brought forth in iniquity, and in sin did my mother conceive me. Behold, you delight in truth in the inward being, and you teach me wisdom in the secret heart
—Ps. 51:5–6

It is time to go further into your inward being, your secret heart. It is a daunting leap, but remember that God will minister to you with his mercy and steadfast love. The power of the Gospel doesn't end in the darkness of your secret heart. Christ takes you through the darkness into the light. He teaches and carries you through the darkness so you can come out on the other side transformed.

David knew his adultery was just the tip of the iceberg when it came to his sin, so he asked God to teach him wisdom in his secret heart. You may have never been this honest before with yourself, but don't waste this huge opportunity to do some significant work on your heart. Now is the time to consider what makes you tick, what has motivated you thus far.

Along with a counselor, ask God to reveal where you have misplaced your identity. What are the underlying issues that made you commit adultery? Spend this season reevaluating your view of things, the effects of your childhood, the sinful habits that led up to the adultery, the failures and the successes of your marriage, and the brokenness you have walked through together. Ask God to show you your weaknesses, the places of temptation, and the idols of your heart. What have you been worshipping rather than God?

David admitted that his desires, thoughts, actions, and plans had been tainted with sin ever since he was conceived. He went back to the beginning, and you need to as well. There hadn't been a time David wasn't trying to be wise in his own eyes. Maybe David's persistent pursuit of truth in his secret heart was why God called him a man after his own heart. Are you willing to be the same type of man?

As the psalm says, God delights to teach us truth in our inward being. God wants you to know your heart more than you do. He does so not to merely show you where you have gone astray, but to draw you near into a deeper relationship with him.

God delights in transforming our lives from the inside out. The Apostle Paul realized that the wisdom of God was none other than Jesus Christ himself: *"Christ Jesus, who became to us wisdom from God, righteousness and sanctification and redemption"* (1 Cor. 1:30).

Wisdom is the practical application of the truth of God. When we grow in our relationship with Jesus by studying his Word, we become wise, and he shapes our decisions and actions according to the truth. When Jesus is our wisdom, Jesus sets us free to really live. John wrote:

> *So Jesus said to the Jews who had believed him, "If you abide in my word, you are truly my disciples, and you will know the truth, and the truth will set you free."... So if the Son sets you free, you will be free indeed* (John 8:31–32, 36).

The freedom Jesus offers is a "freedom from" and a "freedom to." He frees us *from* eternal condemnation, shame, and guilt. At the same time, Jesus frees us *to* walk by faith through the devastating earthly consequences of sin and to live in peace, purity, love, assurance, and joy.

You will have many decisions and choices ahead of you. You need the wisdom of God to guide you and give you the right motivations. There will be tough decisions that may not seem to benefit you, but remember—it's not all about you. You repented of that mindset. You need to think about how to love your spouse and your kids first and foremost. You still have the responsibility to provide and protect them, perhaps even more so now than ever before. You will need to be wise with every move you make. Seek to put them in the best position you can. You can't control how they respond to you, but you can control how you treat them.

You will hit the crossroad of teachability many times

throughout your journey. Other faithful believers can help you gain wisdom and insight at this point. You will need to decide to submit to God's Word and do what he is calling you to do every step of the way. Take heart. Jesus invites you to take his yoke and learn from him. If you come to him, he will give your weary heart rest, so you can keep traveling down the road less traveled. In Matthew, we read:

> *Come to me, all who labor and are heavy laden, and I will give you rest. Take my yoke upon you, and learn from me, for I am gentle and lowly in heart, and you will find rest for your souls. For my yoke is easy, and my burden is light.* (Matt. 11:28–30)

Go in prayer and take Jesus' yoke and learn from him.

O Lord, you are my wisdom, my truth, the very Word of God.

I come to sit at your feet and learn from you. Teach me wisdom in my inmost place. I pray you would search me and see if there is any offensive way in me. Lead me in the path of righteousness. May the meditations of my heart be pleasing in your sight. I admit I am scared to open my heart fully to you and bring to light all the sin and shame that have controlled me for so long. Please lift me out of this mire and set me on your rock. Set me free. Rebuild my life on your Word. Help me to live a life of truth without deception. Topple the idols of my heart that I have set up. Conquer these strongholds in my life. Break my addiction to power, comfort, pleasure, and approval. Be the Master of my life. Put your yoke upon me, so I may walk with you and keep in step with the Spirit. May I be a student of my wife and learn how to love her with an unfailing love. Be my wisdom, Jesus!

In the Name of Truth himself, my wisdom Jesus Christ,
Amen

Personal Thoughts, Questions, and Prayers:

CROSSROAD #8

STUBBORNLY STANDING YOUR GROUND OR RENEWING A WILLING SPIRIT

Prayer

Create in me a clean heart, O God, and renew a right spirit within me. Cast me not away from your presence, and take not your Holy Spirit from me…and uphold me with a willing spirit.

—Psalm 51:10–11, 12b

There are going to be a lot of things required of you on the road less traveled. Your wife will demand things of you. Your kids will require things of you. Your extended family will hold interrogations. Your counselor will create action steps, and your church will challenge you in many ways. Your pride will well up inside you, and you will resist doing these things.

Some days you will even throw up your hands and say, "Enough is enough! I have done all I can do to make things right. I'm finished." When your stiff-neck and bowed chest persists, you must turn to the Lord to give you a willing spirit. It's not that you can't convey your thoughts or hesitation. It's more about the spirit you do it with. How you respond is crucial!

Consider the severity of your betrayal toward your wife and kids. It's not fair for you to demand that they just get over it and deal with the betrayal in days, weeks, or even months. They need time to process what has happened, time to receive your repentance, time to consider how they need to repent, time to handle life in the moment, and time to plan for the future.

You will eventually be able to give your side of the story, but the immediate aftermath of your infidelity is not when you should start making demands. It will only shut down the conversation and lead to more frustration, anger, and distrust. You need to wait on safe opportunities for discussion between you and your wife.

You will need a mediator to have deeper conversations. You must be patient. This is not a sprint. It's an extended marathon. God uses time to work truth and forgiveness into our hearts. His patience leads to salvation, and your marriage is included. A continuing heart of repentance and faith will do wonders in your walk with Christ and in your family.

David prayed for a clean heart and a renewed spirit. You also need a new heart and a renewed spirit. Your adultery didn't just happen out of the blue. Sometimes people do find themselves in the wrong place at the wrong time with the wrong person, but usually an affair has been nurtured along emotionally and physically for some time.

Sin captured your heart, and you were carried away with lustful passion and evil desires. Your heart and spirit have been conformed to these desires, and now you must unbridle them. If you are honest, in your heart of hearts you have still reserved a space for that other woman and the possibility of a future with her.

This space must be eradicated.

Only the Holy Spirit can truly remove it. You need the very Spirit of God to dwell within you, to fill you, and to compel you. You need a spiritual transformation. Paul writes:

> *I appeal to you therefore, brothers, by the mercies of God, to present your bodies as a living sacrifice, holy and acceptable to God, which is your spiritual worship. Do not be conformed to this world, but be transformed by the renewal of your mind, that by testing you may discern what is the will of God, what is good and acceptable and perfect.* (Rom. 12:1–2)

Paul reminds you that you are anchored in the mercies of God. In view of God's mercies, your spiritual act of worship is to offer yourself as a living sacrifice by not allowing your heart to be conformed any longer to the desires of this world but to be transformed by the renewal of your mind. In doing so, you will be willing to follow God's will. Being a living sacrifice involves dying to self and living for Christ. Jesus bids you, *"If anyone would come after me, let him deny himself and take up his cross and follow me"* (Matt. 16:24). You must deny yourself with a willing spirit to thoughtfully consider others' needs above your own. A willing spirit is zealous to do what is good and right.

Your sincere desire should be to willingly do good toward your wife no matter what she decides about the marriage. God will take great pleasure in using you toward this end.

Many men will depart from repentance and faith at this point.

If he doesn't sense that he is going to get what he wants and his wife can't get past the affair, he cuts bait. Out of childish bitterness, he will make the divorce very difficult and short-circuit the legal proceedings. He will throw his wife under the bus. I've seen men try to save face by blaming their actions on the lawyer, saying things like, "My lawyer made me do it." Your lawyer works for you and not the other way around.

Bless your wife:—period.

The way you treat her at this juncture may even be the very thing God uses to soften her heart and bring about healing. But remember that your goal is to honor the Lord and to honor your wife with your actions and not to manipulate an outcome. Go to God holding back nothing, and ask him to transform everything.

O Spirit of the Living God,
Fall afresh on me! Lord, I confess my stubborn heart.
The demands of reconciliation seem insurmountable.
Many nights, I pound my head against the wall
because it seems like it will never be enough. I can't
seem to convince anyone of my sincerity. They don't
trust my words; they don't believe that I mean it.

God, I want to give up, but I know I need to keep moving forward. Give me a willing spirit to keep taking the road least taken. I can see why it is the least taken, because it requires much more than I expected. I know the thoughts I have against my wife are wrong right now, but it seems like she wants to use me as her punching bag. She is still so angry, and I have begun to think we would be better off apart from each other. Fill me with your Spirit to help me not fight with her but to fight for her and our marriage. Don't leave me in this desperation. Walk with me and help me keep in step with the Spirit. Give me a willing spirit to honor you and my wife.
In the name of Jesus, the One who gives the Spirit generously to those who believe,
Amen.

Personal Thoughts, Questions, and Prayers:

CROSSROAD #9

IGNORING THE FALLOUT OR DEALING WITH YOUR REPERCUSSIONS

Prayer

Deliver me from bloodguiltiness, O God.
—Ps. 51:14a

You need to come to the realization that committing adultery has caused a ripple effect of betrayal and pain in the lives of your children, extended family, friendships, coworkers, and church. David's adultery led to lies, murder, abuse of power, and the death of a child. Your adultery is no different. It has caused widespread repercussions. Watch out for making demands that your loved ones can't give you at this moment, especially your kids.

You will need to pray for God to deliver you and those involved from your bloodguiltiness. Asking for forgiveness is just the beginning. You need to pick up the pieces, especially in your kid's lives. You need to take care of their needs.

Your words will only have meaning if they are matched with your deeds of provision, protection, and love. Your kids have been looking to you as their role model of a husband and a father. Your betrayal has rocked their world. They will question your love, your word, and what it even means to be a Christian. Their model of marriage and family has been bulldozed.

They are so confused. They don't even know how to communicate what they are feeling—anger, sadness, loneliness, fear, and betrayal. One child will want things to go back to the way they were. Another child will want to fight. And another child will want to hide. You will need to be patient with them and meet them where they are.

They may need some space from you, because they have been told not to talk to strangers, and I'm sad to say, you are a stranger to them right now. You must rebuild their trust. At this point, the most powerful thing you can do for them is to model a repentant father and husband.

Family events will not be the same for some time. Holidays will be stifled. Birthdays will be awkward. Finances will become a major issue to tackle. Living arrangements will need to be addressed, schedules will become a hassle, and communication will become more important than ever. The way you speak about your spouse to others and in front of the kids will need to be gracious and God-honoring. Counseling will be vital to help you move your relationship forward, as well as your relationship with your children. What you had is gone. You must rebuild a new life.

These are the obvious repercussions, but your adultery

has a much further reach. Consider your sin against the other woman and her family if she has one. Your church family will be distraught and need to be cared for. Your mutual friendships will be tattered. The news of your adultery will pull the band-aids off the wounds of others who have been betrayed. Even though you are no longer under the care of your mother and father, they will grieve over your actions and hurt in a deep way for you. Your wife may need to find a job. Your kids' schooling might need to change. You may need to arrange new living arrangements or sell the house.

You especially need to pray for your wife to be delivered from the repercussions. Her life has just been turned inside out and upside down. You need to pray for God to meet her in her emotional turmoil. You need to pray for her physical stability, from weariness, weeping, and withdrawal. She needs prayer for her mental state as she cares for the kids, works, and maneuvers all the decisions hurled at her. You need to pray for friendships that will step in to uphold her and the counsel she will be offered.

David saw the many ramifications of his sin with Bathsheba that led to the death of Uriah, a trusted mighty man in his army, and the death of his son. It's one thing to wreck your own life, but to bring devastation on those entrusted in your care is enough to undo you. David cried out for deliverance from his bloodguiltiness.

You need to pray for your sons not to follow in your footsteps. You need to pray for them to trust you again as their father. Pray your sin will not cause them to doubt God's goodness and his faithfulness. Much of our understanding of our Heavenly Father is established in our relationship with our earthly father. Pray for stability in their lives as they spend separate time with you and with their mother. Pray you will not discourage them in any way toward their mother.

You need to pray for your daughter. Her little heart is crushed beyond measure, and she will have nightmares that her husband will do this to her. Pray that she will be able to trust men again. Pray she doesn't throw herself into a bad relationship to replace you in her life. Pray against her anger and that she will not pull away from her mother. She has in many ways lost her daddy. Pray she can cry out to her heavenly father, "Abba Father!" in her lonely moments for help.

The hard truth is that you can't make your wife stay in the marriage. You have broken your covenant vows. The marriage trust has been torn asunder.

Jesus has given her permission to leave.

Just as David fasted and prayed while his son still lived, his hope was God might be gracious and see fit to save his son. So you too must wait on the Lord with a contrite heart to see if he will give your wife the faith to not only forgive you but to remain in union with you. David's son did die, and your marriage might die as well.

Whether your marriage lives or dies may depend significantly on your humility as you walk in repentance and faith.

Cry out to God to minimize the effects of your adultery on innocent bystanders especially those under your care.

Abba Father, my deliverer and defender,

Lord, I have made a mess of so many lives from my

selfish actions. As a believer, I was called to fight for others and to defend them from the evil one, but now I have become an evil one. Rescue them from me. Save them from my sin and bloodguilt. Lord, I can't undo what I have done, but you can redeem the ongoing effects of my sin upon my wife, my family, and my friends. Just as David wept and fasted for his son to live, I tear my clothes in ashes and wait upon your mercy for those in my life. God, keep me from doing any more damage. May my words, actions, and interaction from this point forward be part of the healing. Keep the evil one from getting a foothold in their lives and hide them under the shadow of your wings. Minister to them in their innermost places. God, I beg of you, deliver them.

In the name of Jesus, my ever-present help in trouble, Amen.

Personal Thoughts, Questions, and Prayers:

CROSSROAD #10

PROVING YOURSELF WORTHY AGAIN OR OFFERING A BROKEN SPIRIT & CONTRITE HEART

Prayer

For you will not delight in sacrifice, or I would give it; you will not be pleased with a burnt offering. The sacrifices of God are a broken spirit; a broken and contrite heart, O God, you will not despise.
—Ps. 51:16–17

When things don't go your way, you will resort to living like an orphan, as if the Heavenly Father has turned his back on you and disowned you. As a spiritual orphan, you will try to earn God's favor again and to offer all kinds of sacrifices to get his attention. You will try and barter with God: "If I do this and that, you've got to bless me. Look at what I am doing, shouldn't this get me some reprieve?" But God will not accept your good deeds or your zealous efforts as appeasement for your sin. You can't bribe

God. God only wants you. The only sacrifice he will accept is a broken and contrite heart.

He is more concerned with the inner workings of your heart than the outworking of your flesh. If you have made it this far down the road less traveled, you have come to grips with your sin and its devastation. Hopefully, you have come to the end of yourself in surrender. God will accept your surender. You do not have what it takes to fix the mess you've gotten yourself and your family into. The only thing you can bring to the table is a broken and contrite heart over your sin.

He will draw near to you in this humble estate. You can trust God to do immeasurably more than all you ask or think in your brokenness:

> *The LORD is near to the brokenhearted and saves the crushed in spirit.* (Ps. 34:18)

> *A bruised reed he will not break, and a faintly burning wick he will not quench; he will faithfully bring forth justice.* (Isa. 42:3)

Remember, you started with mercy, and you must continue in his mercy and steadfast love. Ultimately, there is nothing you can do to ensure that your marriage will be saved. God is calling your family to sit at the feet of Jesus so he can minister to each one of you. Pray for God to draw near to your wife and to mend your family's crushed spirits. Pray for God to not snuff out the wick of your marriage and to tend to your family's bruised hearts. Acts of kindness with no strings attached and free gifts of grace with no demands will truly bless your wife and family. Your good deeds can't be offered to get your wife or kids or God to do what you want. Love must be your motive and your chief end.

The road less traveled doesn't always end in a reunited marriage, but it does always end with our union in Christ. Being united to Christ will give you the strength to handle what lies around the next bend. Whether you and your wife come out embracing one another, or being co-parents to your children, or going your separate ways, you need to honor the Lord every step of the way. This will take great humility and faith. I've seen God bring healing in so many different outcomes, even where the couple gets divorced but comes back together further down the road. The key is to remain humble in loving your wife and family no matter what path they choose to take.

It will be hard to handle not being in control, and your heart will break in a whole different way. Be assured that the Lord will meet you in your brokenness, and he will not abandon you. Being a bruised reed and a faintly burning wick is a vulnerable state, but God can do some of his most beautiful work in our weakest moments. Paul wanted God to remove the thing that made him weak, but God reminded him of the usefulness of his weakness. Paul writes:

> *But he said to me, "My grace is sufficient for you, for my power is made perfect in weakness." Therefore I will boast all the more gladly of my weaknesses, so that the power of Christ may rest upon me.* (1 Cor. 12:9)

One of the hardest prayers to pray is, "Thy will be done, Lord."

My Emmanuel, draw near to me.
Draw near to my wife and my family. Be our refuge and strength. Hide us in the cleft of the rock from the storm I have caused. Silence the waves of despair that are crushing my wife and my own overwhelming doubts. Give her faith to walk through the pain. Give me peace in the unknown. As Peter sank in the rough waters, grab us and lift us up to safety. Turn our gaze back to you when our circumstances paralyze us in fear. Lord, I want to make things right and mend our marriage, but it doesn't seem to be working. Forgive me if I come with demands both to you and to her. Compel us both with your love. God, I acknowledge I can't bring an offering or a sacrifice to you. You are not impressed with what I can do but with my weakness before you. All I have is my broken spirit and contrite heart. I give it to you. Have your way with me. Thy will be done in my marriage and my family. I will trust you no matter the outcome.
In the name of Jesus, the one broken for me,
Amen.

Personal Thoughts, Questions, and Prayers:

CROSSROAD #11

MAKING THIS ALL ABOUT YOURSELF OR OPENING YOUR LIFE UP TO HELP SINNERS

Prayer

Then I will teach transgressors your ways, and sinners will return to you.... O God of my salvation, and my tongue will sing aloud of your righteousness. O Lord, open my lips, and my mouth will declare your praise.
—Ps. 51:13, 14b–15

I have sat across the table from many men who, years after their adultery, didn't believe God could ever use them again to minister to others. They were deflated and felt they had lost all credibility to speak into anyone's life. Some had rightly lost their credentials to be pastors. Some were removed from the office of elder and deacon. Some were on their second marriages.

You may lose the privilege to lead in some positions, but you are not disqualified to minister to others. God does not waste our sin, brokenness, or our struggles. He uses them in his ministry of the Gospel.

You may need to take the bench for a season, but your journey down the road of repentance and faith can be a useful tool as a warning in the lives of the next generation. Your testimony can halt fellow sinners from plunging further into a similar path of destruction. Your story can speak to a friend who may be contemplating an affair. Your journey of repentance and faith is not limited to those in sexual sin either. There is no sin that is not common to people. Your redemption can be translated into almost any struggle with sin. The question is: Are you willing to be used by God in this way?

It will take vulnerability and humility to share your sin with others. David wrote Psalm 51 for all sinners. He gave it to the choirmaster to be put to music and sung in church.

If you're like me, I'm not sure I'm ready to have my most grievous sins sung at church, but I do know that God uses sinners like you and me in the lives of other sinners. David got to the point where he wanted to be used to turn sinners back into a right relationship with God. Instead of sinning from his rooftop, he now shouts the praises of God from the rooftops.

Ask your pastor if there is anyone you could help on the road of repentance and faith. Lean into people's lives and into the challenges they are facing. Be open for God to use you to teach transgressors the way less traveled.

Ask God to use you and your story for his glory.

O Lord, the one who makes beauty out of ashes,

God, it is hard for me to even lift my head some days. I profoundly doubt that you can use me as an instrument in your hand. I can understand being an instrument of wickedness, but to be an instrument of righteousness again is too lofty for me to consider. Lord, even in my doubt, I pray that if you could use my story to turn one sinner back to you, then I will be your crooked stick to point the way. Give me confidence in you and not in myself to speak forth the truth boldly, to own my sin before others, and even more so to own your saving grace before others. I would have preferred to be used as the right way to live rather than what to avoid, but nonetheless, use me as you see fit. Take my sin and use it for your glory and the benefit of your people.

In the name of Jesus, the best friend of sinners,

Amen.

Personal Thoughts, Questions, and Prayers:

CROSSROAD #12

DISMISSING THE CHURCH BODY OR DOING GOOD AND BUILDING HER UP

Prayer

Do good to Zion in your good pleasure; build up the walls of Jerusalem; then will you delight in right sacrifices.
—Ps. 51:18–19a

As we come to the twelfth crossroad, I want to circle back around to the friend I mentioned at the beginning of the book. After some deep personal repentance, he came to the conclusion he needed to confess his sin to the congregation. So the next Sunday, both he and his wife came before the church and confessed their sin. They each humbly told our church family how they had sinned against God, each other, and the church body.

As they wept and asked for forgiveness, the church rose to their feet and gathered around them in Christ's steadfast love and abundant mercy. We prayed over them and committed to walking with them as they sought reconciliation in their marriage. It was a glorious and beautiful moment for our church—a true gift of God. Just as the psalmist prayed in Psalm 51, their journey of repentance and faith was good for Zion (the church) and built us up. Their vulnerability and willingness "to confess their sins one to another" was powerful for their marriage and for all those in attendance that day. We all experienced the balm of the Gospel deep within our hearts, especially those who had been affected by adultery themselves.

The evil one will lie to you and tell you the church is against you, the church will only judge you, and the church will never forgive you. Remember the devil is the Father of Lies.

It is a lie.

The road less traveled is a road that includes the church. I pray you are in a church that will walk with you and your wife through repentance and faith. The road taken by most though leads away from the church, and most usually never darken its doors again. They remain in their shame and embarrassment. The church needs you, and it needs to see Christ's gracious reconciliation in your life.

Many of our members went home that day and began talking about their need to nurture their relationship and guard their own marriage. The next week, our small group was surprisingly more vulnerable about their sin. They shared past experiences where God had granted them much grace to walk in repentance and faith as well. Our church will never be the same because this couple was willing to let us join them on the road less traveled.

The discipline of the church is meant to be restorative. It

is for the good of the children of God. It shows that God loves us, and he wants what is best for us. Trust in the Lord and submit yourself to the discipline of the body of Christ. Ask God to use the church in this process and to use you to build her up.

Jesus, head of the Church,
Everything in me wants to avoid the scrutiny of the church. I don't want to go to worship, and I don't want to face my brothers and sisters in the Lord. They won't understand; I fear their judgment. I can't entrust myself into their hands. It's none of their business anyway, right? I want to just slip away and not deal with it. God, I need you to walk with me into their presence. I may even need you to carry me. Help me to confess my sin before my brothers and sisters that our relationship may be reconciled. Let my repentance be a balm to their soul and bring healing to the wounds only you know about. Help me to do good in my confession, a right sacrifice pleasing to you. Let me be an instrument to build up the church and to not tear it down. Let me do good to my wife, who is your daughter and a member of your church, your beloved in Christ. May I be a blessing especially to her from this day forward.
In the name of Jesus, the bridegroom of the church,
Amen.

Personal Thoughts, Questions, and Prayers

A FINAL WORD OF HOPE

I hope this book has ministered to your heart and given you much to think about. Even more, I pray it has given you hope: hope for your own walk with Christ, hope for your marriage, and hope for your family. I know it is a tough road, and each step is crucial. Stay the course. Run the race Christ has marked out for you. May he show you and your wife favor and grace.

Here is one last encouraging thought. Right now you are in the thick of your adultery, but I want you to get a glimpse of the hope God has in store for you. You have looked at David's darkest night, but God made something beautiful out of those ashes. God took David's sin with Bathsheba and transformed it into a story of redemption. His story is not just an Old Testament side story, but a huge part of THE STORY.

David, Bathsheba, and their son Solomon are counted among the lineage of Jesus given in Matthew. After David and Bathsheba's first son dies, Bathsheba gives birth to

Solomon, who was given the name Jedidiah, the beloved of the Lord.

> *...and Jesse the father of David the king. And David was the father of Solomon by the wife of Uriah, ...and Jacob the father of Joseph the husband of Mary, of whom Jesus was born, who is called Christ.* (Matt. 1:6, 16)

By God's grace, Jesus can make something beautiful out of your ashes. Through your repentance and faith, you can be restored to the family of Jesus.

He could even call you a man after God's own heart.

A PASTOR'S PRAYER

So they are no longer two but one flesh.
What therefore God has joined together, let not man separate.
—Matt. 19:6

Count it all joy, my brothers, when you meet trials of various kinds.
—James 1:2

One of my greatest joys as a pastor is doing premarital counseling. The conversations are filled with giddiness, excitement, expectation, and honesty. The rehearsal dinners are a tremendous joy. The family and friends tell stories of God's providential handiwork in knitting the two lovebirds together. The wedding is a one-of-a-kind type of joy, an extravagant taste of heaven. God invites all in attendance to peer into the mystery of the Gospel, where Christ takes his bride for himself, and a kiss unites time and eternity forever. Vows are given, symbols of undying love are exchanged, and a pronouncement is made of God's approval and power to bind husband and wife together as one!

All these are an amazing privilege to experience, but the culmination of my joy resides in watching a couple journey faithfully together face-to-face, hand-in-hand, and shoulder-to-shoulder with Christ year after year and decade after decade until they find their seat at the Wedding Feast of the Lamb.

After years of ministry, I've walked many couples through various kinds of trials,—sickness, loss of a loved one, anxiety, financial struggles, doubt, imprisonment, and parenting struggles. Through these trials, I see why James urges us to count it all joy because these trials produce steadfastness and perfect us one degree of glory to the next.

But walking a couple through the trial of adultery? It is hard for me to count it as joy. I wish I could tell young pastors this will be a rare ministerial occurrence, but research shows that 50 percent of first time marriages end in divorce, predominantly due to infidelity. The American Psychological Association research reveals that 42 percent of all divorcees reported more than one extramarital sexual contact during the course of their marriages.[1] I'm sad to say that every pastor will face the issue of adultery in their tenure of ministry.

Like everyone else attending wedding ceremonies, I used to ignore the little phrase, "What therefore God hath joined together, let no one tear asunder." I always thought, "No, not these two! No way!" But now I've realized no one is exempt from the deception of their own hearts, the socially accepted promiscuity of our culture, and the weakness of the flesh. This ever-increasing reality has driven me to my knees in prayer for my own marriage, the couples in our church, and the marriages of my friends and community.

This little phrase is not a contrived warning. It's the very warning of Scripture.

Why did God have to say it? Because there will inevitably be all kinds of temptations and trials that will try and tear your marriage apart. The church leaders of Jesus' day (the Pharisees) took divorce lightly, but Jesus and his disciples spoke very seriously about sexual immorality. This should give us great trepidation to pray and to gird up our loins from the specific sin of sexual immorality.

It only takes witnessing one couple you married weeping over sexual betrayal to understand the gravity of this sin. The assault on the soul is excruciating. The lies are devastating. The shame is paralyzing. The distrust is shattering. Even though this sin is utterly crushing, it is not an unforgivable sin and many a marriage has been redeemed and restored through much grace and discipleship. I have seen first hand what God can do if the husband and wife humble themselves before God and one another in repentance, forgiveness, faith, and love.

Like others who try to comfort, confront, and counsel friends through adultery, I have searched for helpful resources to guide me. I needed a resource that was biblical, concise, easy to read, and decisive.

This is why I wrote this book. I want to give the adulterer something he can read in a few hours but also something to meditate on throughout his journey with someone.

The beauty of Psalm 51 is that it addresses the crossroads an adulterer will face, and it offers twelve prayers to guide one's heart, mind, and soul down the road of repentance and faith. I hope this resource will be useful to your ministry as you journey down the road less traveled with couples.

As you noticed, I wrote it for husbands who have committed adultery. I'm sure it is applicable for wives who have committed adultery, too, but I wrote with a very specific audience in mind. This is just an initial resource, and it should be accompanied by other more thorough books and the help of a trained Christian counselor. May the Lord bless you as you extend the abounding mercy and steadfast love of Christ.

I leave you, who are called to champion the fidelity of marriage, with one last prayer—a pastoral prayer for newlyweds.

Lord, the lover of our souls,
What you are joining together today, let not this husband, nor this wife, nor anyone else tear it apart.
May you bind them heart, mind, body and soul together as one, so they are no longer two but one.
By your grace Lord, grant them faithfulness to you, to their own conscience, and to each other.
Transform their disposition of seeking to contentment. May their satisfaction be in you. May they passionately lose themselves in one another's arms.
Astound them with your divine joy that is not of this

world. May there never be a moment they question your love and their love for each other.

O Lord, be their strength and their refuge, an ever-present help in times of trouble. Be the lifter of their heads that they do not get too discouraged to doubt your presence, nor too high that they forget their need for your power. Do not lead them into temptation with wandering eyes or the lusts of the flesh. Make a covenant with their eyes not to sin against you. Keep them from evil! May husband and wife know each other's weaknesses so to not tread where sin is sure to be lurking.

When Lady Folly seductively whispers from the side street, may they run as Joseph from the trap of Potiphar's wife. With fear and trembling, may he flee his youthful lusts as to not dishonor Your Name nor his Beloved's. Let no emotional tie with another tickle her ears to question his undying love for her. May their love not be confined to their thoughts but expressed daily in word and deed. Humble them to put the needs of each other above their own. And when they fail each other and sin against each other, may your kindness lead them to repentance, confessing their sin one to another. May vulnerability and self-disclosure be the warmth they bask in. May they not get so wearied in their labors that they bypass one another in the hectic pace of life. Help them to find rest for their souls as they pray together, read your Word together, and worship together.

Use their home as a beacon of hospitality and mercy to

the sojourner. Surround them with a body of believers that will embrace them as brothers and sisters in grace. Fill them with your Spirit so they may walk in a manner worthy of the Gospel united as one with you. For your name's sake, fill their quiver for generations to come. May their grey hair and wrinkled smiles be a crown and testimony of their covenant faithfulness.
In Jesus' name, our faithful bridegroom,
Amen.

FURTHER SCRIPTURE REFLECTION & RESOURCES

Luke 15:11–32

And he said, "There was a man who had two sons. [12] And the younger of them said to his father, 'Father, give me the share of property that is coming to me.' And he divided his property between them. [13] Not many days later, the younger son gathered all he had and took a journey into a far country, and there he squandered his property in reckless living. [14] And when he had spent everything, a severe famine arose in that country, and he began to be in need. [15] So he went and hired himself out to one of the citizens of that country, who sent him into his fields to feed pigs. [16] And he was longing to be fed with the pods that the pigs ate, and no one gave him anything.

[17] "But when he came to himself, he said, 'How many of my father's hired servants have more than enough bread, but I perish here with hunger! [18] I will arise and go to my father, and I will say to him, "Father, I have sinned against heaven and before you. [19] I am no longer worthy to be called your son. Treat me as one of your hired servants."' [20] And he arose and came to his father. But while

he was still a long way off, his father saw him and felt compassion, and ran and embraced him and kissed him. [21] And the son said to him, 'Father, I have sinned against heaven and before you. I am no longer worthy to be called your son.' [22] But the father said to his servants, 'Bring quickly the best robe, and put it on him, and put a ring on his hand, and shoes on his feet. [23] And bring the fattened calf and kill it, and let us eat and celebrate. [24] For this my son was dead, and is alive again; he was lost, and is found.' And they began to celebrate.

[25] "Now his older son was in the field, and as he came and drew near to the house, he heard music and dancing. [26] And he called one of the servants and asked what these things meant. [27] And he said to him, 'Your brother has come, and your father has killed the fattened calf, because he has received him back safe and sound.' [28] But he was angry and refused to go in. His father came out and entreated him, [29] but he answered his father, 'Look, these many years I have served you, and I never disobeyed your command, yet you never gave me a young goat, that I might celebrate with my friends. [30] But when this son of yours came, who has devoured your property with prostitutes, you killed the fattened calf for him!' [31] And he said to him, 'Son, you are always with me, and all that is mine is yours.

[32] It was fitting to celebrate and be glad, for this your brother was dead, and is alive; he was lost, and is found.'"

Proverbs 5

[1] My son, be attentive to my wisdom; incline your ear to my understanding,

[2] that you may keep discretion, and your lips may guard knowledge.

[3] For the lips of a forbidden woman drip honey, and her speech is smoother than oil,

[4] but in the end she is bitter as wormwood, sharp as a two-edged sword.

[5] Her feet go down to death; her steps follow the path to Sheol;

[6] she does not ponder the path of life; her ways wander, and she does not know it.

[7] And now, O sons, listen to me, and do not depart from the words of my mouth.

[8] Keep your way far from her, and do not go near the door of her house,

[9] lest you give your honor to others and your years to the merciless,

[10] lest strangers take their fill of your strength, and your labors go to the house of a foreigner,

[11] and at the end of your life you groan, when your flesh and body are consumed,

[12] and you say, "How I hated discipline, and my heart despised reproof!

[13] I did not listen to the voice of my teachers or incline my ear to my instructors.

[14] I am at the brink of utter ruin in the assembled congregation."

[15] Drink water from your own cistern, flowing water from your own well.

[16] Should your springs be scattered abroad, streams of water in the streets?

[17] Let them be for yourself alone, and not for strangers with you.

[18] Let your fountain be blessed, and rejoice in the wife of your youth,

[19] a lovely deer, a graceful doe. Let her breasts fill you at all times with delight; be intoxicated always in her love.

[20] Why should you be intoxicated, my son, with a forbidden woman and embrace the bosom of an adulteress?

[21] For a man's ways are before the eyes of the LORD, and he ponders all his paths.

[22] The iniquities of the wicked ensnare him, and he is held fast in the cords of his sin.

[23] He dies for lack of discipline, and because of his great folly he is led astray.

John 8:1–11

[1] But Jesus went to the Mount of Olives. [2] Early in the morning he came again to the temple. All the people came to him, and he sat down and taught them. [3] The scribes and the Pharisees brought a woman who had been caught in adultery, and placing her in the midst [4] they said to him, "Teacher, this woman has been caught in the act of adultery. [5] Now in the Law, Moses commanded us to stone such women. So what do you say?" [6] This they said to test him, that they might have some charge to bring against him. Jesus bent down and wrote with his finger on the ground. [7] And as they continued to ask him, he stood up and said to them, "Let him who is without sin among you be the first to throw a stone at her." [8] And once more he bent down and wrote on the ground. [9] But when they heard it, they went away one by one, beginning with the older ones, and Jesus was left alone with the woman standing before him. [10] Jesus stood up and said to her, "Woman, where are they? Has no one condemned you?" [11] She said, "No one, Lord." And Jesus said, "Neither do I condemn you; go, and from now on sin no more."

Luke 7:36–50

[36] One of the Pharisees asked him to eat with him, and he went into the Pharisee's house and reclined at table. [37] And behold, a woman of the city, who was a sinner, when she learned that he was reclining at table in the Pharisee's house, brought an alabaster flask of ointment, [38] and standing behind him at his feet, weeping, she began to wet his feet with her tears and wiped them with the hair of her head and kissed his feet and anointed them with the ointment. [39] Now when the Pharisee who had invited him saw this, he said to himself, "If this man were a prophet, he would have known who and what sort of woman this is who is touching him, for she is a sinner." [40] And Jesus answering said to him, "Simon, I have something to say to you." And he answered, "Say it, Teacher."

[41] "A certain moneylender had two debtors. One owed five hundred denarii, and the other fifty. [42] When they could not pay, he cancelled the debt of both. Now which of them will love him more?" [43] Simon answered, "The one, I suppose, for whom he cancelled the larger debt." And he said to him, "You have judged rightly." [44] Then turning toward the woman he said to Simon, "Do you see this woman? I entered your house; you gave me no water for my feet, but she has wet my feet with her tears and wiped them with her hair. [45] You gave me no kiss, but from the time I came in she has not ceased to kiss my feet. [46] You did not anoint my head with oil, but she has anointed my feet with ointment. [47] Therefore I tell you, her sins, which are many, are forgiven—for she loved much. But he who is forgiven little, loves little." [48] And he said to her, "Your sins are forgiven." [49] Then those who were at table with him began to say among themselves, "Who is this, who even forgives sins?" [50] And he said to the woman, "Your faith has saved you; go in peace."

RESOURCES

www.bradhambrick.com
(Online counseling resources)

www.ccef.org
(Christian Counseling & Educational Foundation)

Every Man's Battle: Winning the War on Sexual Temptation One Victory at a Time (The Every Man Series) by Stephen Arterburn and Fred Stoeker

The Christian Man by Patrick Morley

The Complete Husband by Lou Priolo

Sacred Marriage by Gary Thomas

The Meaning of Marriage by Timothy and Kathy Keller

After an Affair: Pursuing Restoration (31-Day Devotionals for Life) by Michael Scott Gembola

Fighting for Your Marriage by Linda Rooks

The Soul of Shame by Curt Thompson

Shame Interrupted by Edward Welch

Together Through The Storms by Jeff and Sara Walton

Intimate Allies by Dan Allender and Tremper Longman III

NOTES

At the Crossroads

1. "The Hound of Heaven" is a 1893 poem by Francis Thompson, where Thompson compares God's loving, relentless pursuit of sinners to that of a hound.

Crossroad #3

1. Alexander MacLaren, *The Expositor's Bible: The Psalms, Volume 2*, (New York: Hodder and Stoughton, 2013), 139.

A Pastor's Prayer

1. Rebeca A. Martin, Andrew Christensen, and David C. Atkins, "Infidelity and Behavioral Couple Therapy: Relationship Outcomes Over 5 Years Following Therapy" *American Psychological Association* 3, no. 1 (2014), 1.

Follow Kevin's writings and work at

www.kevinthumpston.com

www.ingramcontent.com/pod-product-compliance
Lightning Source LLC
LaVergne TN
LVHW020048110826
845155LV00029B/684

* 9 7 8 1 9 5 1 9 9 1 1 2 8 *